MW00510290

New Psalms for New Moms

A KEEPSAKE JOURNAL

LINDA ANN OLSON

May the Lord richly bless both you and your children.
—Psalm 115:14

JUDSON PRESS VALLEY FORGE

New Psalms for New Moms: A Keepsake Journal

Library of Congress Cataloging-in-Publication Data

Olson, Linda Ann
New psalms for new moms : a keepsake journal / Linda Ann Olson
p. cm.
ISBN 0-8170-1298-2 (alk. paper)
1. Mothers — Prayers-book and devotions — English. 2. Spiritual journals. 3. Title.
BV4847.057 1999
242'.6431 — dc21 98-53387

Printed in the U.S.A.
06 05 04 03 02 01 00 99
10 9 8 7 6 5 4 3 2 1

Dedicated with love to my mother, Cecilia;
my husband, Carl;
and our two gifts from God,
our sons Brent David and Jeffrey Carl.

Contents

Introduction

Here is a place to record your own private conversations with God as you and your baby encounter all the joys and challenges ahead. Each mother's journey is wonderfully unique, filled with personal triumphs, doubts, dreams, and prayers. Make this your book by using the journal entries to stimulate and guide, but not limit, your reflections. When you've filled this book with all the yearnings of a new mother's heart, it will be a cherished keepsake like no other. May this prayer journal be a blessing to both you and your family.

Linda Ann Olson

Good things come to those who wait

Am I or Not?

Lord, I have been living in sweet suspense.
There has been nothing else on my mind for days.
Am I pregnant or not?
Today I found out for sure.
The answer is yes!
I'm exhilarated.
I'm scared.
There is no turning back now.
I'm on the road to becoming a mom.
Together, Lord, we're going to have a baby!

~

"And anyone who welcomes a little child like this on my behalf is welcoming me." — *Matthew 18:5*

My Journal

~

YESTERDAY

When I was a little girl, I thought the best thing about being a mother would be . . .

My Journal

~

TODAY

Now that I know for sure I'm pregnant, my prayer is that . . .

My Journal

~

Tomorrow

I'm going to pray each day during my pregnancy that my baby will be . . .

Why Do I Feel So Bad When Our News Is So Good?

Heavenly Father, I loved the excitement
of telling all our family and friends that we're expecting!
We've spread our personal good news far and wide.
I don't think I've ever been hugged so many times.
But that part of this adventure is past.
Now I'm facing the daily reality of morning sickness
(which should be called morning, afternoon, and evening sickness).
Even the sight of certain foods makes me queasy.
I'm told that this, too, shall pass.
I hope it passes quickly!
Lord, help me get through this part of the process.

~

"So be strong and take courage, all you who put your hope in the LORD!" —Psalm 31:24

"We can rejoice, too, when we run into problems and trials, for we know that they are good for us — they help us learn to endure." —Romans 5:3

My Journal

~

YESTERDAY

A mother I've always admired and would like to emulate is . . .

My Journal

~

TODAY

Instead of thinking about this morning sickness, I'll concentrate on . . .
A Bible verse that inspires me now is . . .

My Journal

~

Tomorrow

The first thing I'm going to do when I start to feel better again is . . .

The Blessing of Health Care

Thank you, Lord, for the medical care
that I am receiving throughout my pregnancy.
I'm sadly aware that this is not always available.
I believe that those of us who enjoy this vital service are called
to help make it a reality for women and children everywhere.
Thank you for the doctors, nurses, and other health-care providers
who are there for me each step of the way.
Thank you for the technology
that detects problems and helps solve them.
Thank you for the knowledge and expertise of the medical community.
Most of all, Lord, thank you for this beautiful new life
that is growing day by day inside me.

~

"You made all the delicate, inner parts of my body and knit me together in my mother's womb. Thank you for making me so wonderfully complex! Your workmanship is marvelous — and how well I know it. You watched me as I was being formed in utter seclusion, as I was woven together in the dark of the womb."
—Psalm 139:13-15

My Journal

~

Yesterday

My biggest health concerns in the past were . . .

My Journal

TODAY

I'm taking really good care of myself and my baby by . . .

My Journal

~

Tomorrow

I'm praying especially for the following people who are taking care of me during these nine months . . .

Patience Is a Virtue (I Haven't Acquired Yet)

Lord, now that I am getting closer to delivering this baby,
my patience is starting to unravel like a piece of cloth
that has been stretched too far.
Patience has never been easy for me.
This time of anticipation and preparation is a time to slow down
and discover the virtue of patience.
Lord, I know that patience is high on the list of qualities for a mother
as she responds to the constant needs of a newborn infant.
Develop this quality in me each day
as I wait for the birth of this baby.

~

"Praise the LORD, O Jerusalem! Praise your God, O Zion! For he has fortified the bars of your gates and blessed your children within you." —Psalm 147:12-13

"But when the Holy Spirit controls our lives, he will produce this kind of fruit in us: love, joy, peace, patience, kindness, goodness, faithfulness, gentleness and self control." —Galatians 5: 22-23

My Journal

~

Yesterday

There were times in the past when I practiced patience, such as . . .

My Journal

TODAY

Someone who is a good role model of patience for me is . . .

My Journal

TOMORROW

Three ways I can help my child learn patience are . . .

The Gift of Prayer

Thank you, God, for the powerful gift of prayer!
No matter how low my spirits,
they are lifted up when I lift my problems to you.
Our daily conversations are a great source of strength and comfort to me
as I go through this waiting time.
Each month is filled with new growth and new questions.
I know that you are waiting with me.
Yes, you are always by my side.
As I sit in the waiting room at the doctor's office,
I enjoy this quiet time talking with you, O Lord.
I find that this experience of becoming a mother is bringing me
closer and closer to you, the Creator of us all.

~

"Devote yourselves to prayer with an alert mind and a thankful heart." —Colossians 4:2

"Don't worry about anything; instead, pray about everything. Tell God what you need, and thank him for all he has done." —Philippians 4:6

My Journal

~

Yesterday

The most powerful prayer experience I had in the past was . . .

My Journal

~

TODAY

A prayer that inspires me now is . . .

My Journal

~

Tomorrow

Two things I'm going to do to strengthen my prayer life in the years ahead are . . .

Nine Months and Counting

As I come to the last month of pregnancy,
I feel a special kinship with the Virgin Mary.
I try to imagine how patiently she made the bumpy trip to Bethlehem,
wondering about the God-child she carried within.
I fully understand the meaning of "heavy with child."
I feel enormous and awkward and ready to burst.
(I even need maternity shoes!)
I am so uncomfortable that sleeping is a real challenge.
I'm ready physically to end this first part of motherhood,
but I'm still not sure I'm prepared.
It isn't the baby's room that concerns me.
Or the strange and sweet items
that have been filling our home for the last few months.
It's me.
Am I ready to be a mother?
Will I do a good job?
Will our baby be healthy?
How will we handle all the changes this means in our lives?

The questions just go round and round in my mind.
Help me not to give in to panic but to trust steadfastly in you.
O Lord, I ask for your blessing on me and this child
and the grace and courage to accept whatever may come.

~

"His righteous acts will be told to those yet unborn."
—Psalm 22:31

"So don't worry about tomorrow, for tomorrow will bring its own worries." *—Matthew 6:34*

My Journal

~

YESTERDAY

One of the best things I have learned from my own mother is . .

My Journal

~

TODAY

My major concern about becoming a mother is . . .

My Journal

~

TOMORROW

A helpful book that I'm going to read in preparation for becoming a good parent is . . .

Ready or Not, Here I Come!

This is the moment I have both yearned for
and dreaded for months, Lord.
We're on the way to end this long pregnancy
and begin the incredible challenge of raising a child.
Help me remember all the childbirth classes.
Please calm my fears and nerves.
The force of this new life has completely taken over my body.
It's both awesome and frightening.
Nothing has prepared me for the force of these contractions.
I'm so exhausted. I can't remember when I had a full night's sleep.
Please stay with me, Lord; I've never needed you more than now.
Guide my doctors and nurses, helping them make the right decisions.
I pray that my baby and I will get through the delivery in good health.

~

"My help comes from the LORD, who made the heavens and the earth!"
—Psalm 121:2

"Listen closely to my prayer, O LORD; hear my urgent cry.
I will call to you whenever trouble strikes, and you will answer me."
—Psalm 86:6-7

My Journal

YESTERDAY

One of the stories I remember being told about my own birth is . . .

My Journal

~

TODAY

I'll never forget that trip to the hospital because . . .

My Journal

~

TOMORROW

What I'm really looking forward to when we get home is . . .

We Did It!

Father of us all, I can't begin to describe
how I felt when I first held this newborn baby —
the tremendous relief of being delivered from my cumbersome body
and the joy of holding a brand-new life.
Suddenly, I felt a kinship with women throughout the ages,
even, in a very small way, with Mary, the mother of Jesus.
I looked back and glimpsed all the generations
who have brought me to this point.
I looked ahead to all the generations to come.
All are part of your majestic plan.
And yet, at the same time, I feel as if I'm the only woman
who has ever accomplished this wondrous thing.
I've stepped into my small place on the continuum of life,
giddy with an overwhelming sense of life and love.
Life! The most powerful force in the universe.
I know now that when a baby is delivered,
It's not a boy.
It's not a girl.
It's a miracle!

~

"And his mother stored all these things in her heart." —Luke 2:51

"Then he took the children into his arms and placed his hands on their heads and blessed them." —Mark 10:16

My Journal

~

YESTERDAY

The first time I really felt like a mother was . . .

My Journal

~

TODAY

The first time I held you I thought . . .

My Journal

~

TOMORROW

The first person I'm going to call to announce your birth is . . .

Part Two

Now We're a Family

The 2:00 A.M. Feeding

The Gift of Sleep

Faithful Friends

One of Those Days!

Rocking to Sleep

When My Baby Is Sick

Calling All Angels!

Motherhood day by day

Now We're a Family

My baby and I are home from the hospital now, Lord,
and our new life as a family has begun. Nothing will ever be the same!
Everything looks as it did before, yet so very different.
The things that were so important to me before,
like the perfect picture for over the sofa or the just-right pair of curtains,
seem insignificant now.
We have brought the most valuable addition to our home — new life.
Everything else pales by comparison.
Even our cat, who ruled with an iron paw,
must now take a back seat to this new creation.
Help us focus on what really matters
and not worry over the details of everyday life, O Lord.
We made so many decisions before, big and small,
and so many investments in our lives and home.
Now we are investing our time, energy, resources — our very selves —
into this small miracle. Now we are investing in life. And life is eternal.

~

"For God so loved the world that he gave his only Son, so that everyone who believes in him will not perish but have eternal life."
—John 3:16

"I said to the LORD, 'You are my Master! All the good things I have are from you.' " *—Psalm 16:2*

My Journal

~

Yesterday

All the way home with you, our new baby, I thought of . . .

My Journal

~

Today

The people who greeted us when we brought you home were . . .

My Journal

~

Tomorrow

I'm going to sing to you my favorite song when I was a child, which is . . .

The 2:00 A.M. Feeding

Lord, help me respond willingly and lovingly
to the cries of this helpless infant you have entrusted to my care.
I am so tired!
Sometimes one day blends into the next
with only scant patches of sleep to refresh me.
With your help and the loving support of family and friends,
I will find my strength in your unending strength,
my inner peace in the deepest peace you offer to all who seek you.
My baby is fed and dry and once again at peace.
He is so beautiful in his trusting slumber.
Help me remember this precious moment of solitude we are sharing
when his cries pierce the quiet night again . . . at 4:00 A.M.!

~

"Love is patient and kind . . . Love never gives up, never loses faith, is always hopeful, and endures through every circumstance."
—1 Corinthians 13:4-7

"Now I can rest again, for the LORD has been so good to me."
—Psalm 116:7

My Journal

~

YESTERDAY

In the past, my experience in taking care of babies included . . .

My Journal

~

TODAY

To cope with these difficult times, I'm going to enlist the help of . . .

A baby-care book that I turn to for information is . . .

My Journal

~

Tomorrow

I'm going to look back and smile about this some day (really) but until then, I'll . . .

The Gift of Sleep

Sleep is something I used to take for granted, Lord!
Now it is on my mind daily.
I long for it like an incredible luxury.
Will I ever enjoy eight hours of uninterrupted sleep at night again?
I pray that our baby will soon begin sleeping through the night.
I know that our days together will be better
if both of us are getting enough sleep.
Until then, please stay with me
through the wee hours of the night
as I feed and change the baby
as if in a dream.
Thank you, Lord, for the gift of refreshing sleep.

~

"I will lie down in peace and sleep, for you alone, O LORD, will keep me safe." —Psalm 4:8

My Journal

~

Yesterday

Another time in my life when I coped with loss of sleep was . . .

My Journal

TODAY

One of the things I can do to help get some sleep during the day is . . .

My Journal

~

Tomorrow

I can help establish healthy sleep patterns for my baby by keeping to a regular schedule and . . .

Faithful Friends

Lord, good friends are a blessing all through our lives,
but never more so than when we call on them in times of need.
I am so grateful for the friends who are keeping me company
on this journey of new motherhood.
I'm especially thankful for the encouragement of experienced mothers
who can guide and comfort me with all my minor trials and tribulations.
Thank you also for friends who share my faith in you,
so that we can pray together and seek strength from your Holy Scriptures.
Every journey, O Lord, is a little smoother
when we're accompanied by a caring, faithful friend.

~

"A friend is always loyal, and a brother is born to help in time of need." —Proverbs 17:17

"How wonderful it is, how pleasant, when brothers live together in harmony!" —Psalm 133:1

"So encourage each other and build each other up, just as you are already doing." —1 Thessalonians 5:11

My Journal

~

Yesterday

My best friend when I was a girl was . . .

My Journal

~

TODAY

The friends I count on the most right now are . . .

My Journal

~

Tomorrow

Two things I'm going to do to be a better friend to others when they need me in the years ahead are . . .

One of Those Days!

O Lord, it's been one of those days.
One small crisis after another since my baby got up
(after hardly sleeping at all last night!).
Help me cope with crying that I cannot seem to stop.
I'm frustrated that I don't know what the problem is,
so I can't begin to solve it.
Is this the dreaded colic I've read about in my baby books?
Please remind me, Lord, to walk away and take a deep breath
when my frustration overtakes my good judgment.
I want to respond lovingly, but sometimes it's so hard, like today.
Why can't the child I love so much and I get along?
Today he didn't want his bottle, cried even after I changed each wet diaper,
didn't want to be held but didn't want to be put down.
Even the cat is in hiding!
I ask for your patience and guidance, Lord, for days like today.
Forgive me when I fail. Help me do better next time.
But, Lord, could we please put off another "one of those days"
for a long, long time?

~

"I love you, LORD; you are my strength." —*Psalm 18:1*

My Journal

~

YESTERDAY

In the past, I've handled frustrating situations by . . .

My Journal

TODAY

Whenever I have "one of those days," I know I can always talk to . . .

My Journal

~

Tomorrow

The next time it looks like a bad day is brewing, I'm going to take a deep breath and say this prayer . . .

Rocking to Sleep

This is the kind of moment that a mother dreams of, Lord.
All is at peace, and she and her baby can gently rock the world away
as they enfold one another in a private, safe cocoon.
As I look down on this trusting little face,
I pray that your protection will always surround him.
His soft gurgling and rhythmic breathing
are like a secret lullaby that only he and I will share.
I hear the ticking of the clock and the creaking of this rocking chair
that once rocked me when I was a baby.
Thank you for the gift of this moment, Lord.
Help me treasure this peace and tranquility.

~

"Let the children come to me. Don't stop them! For the Kingdom of God belongs to such as these. I assure you, anyone who doesn't have their kind of faith will never get into the Kingdom of God."
— Mark 10:14-15

"Look at those who are honest and good, for a wonderful future lies before those who love peace." —Psalm 37:37

My Journal

~

Yesterday

The quiet times I liked best when I was small include . . .

My Journal

TODAY

As we share a moment of bonding, I pray over my baby that he will always . . .

My Journal

~

TOMORROW

I'm going to make sure that we have as many quiet moments together as possible by . . .

When My Baby Is Sick

I feel so helpless today, Lord, because my baby is sick.
She is listless and feels so hot to the touch.
It's frustrating that I cannot do anything except hold her
and give her the medicine the doctor prescribed.
She's so small!
I pray that her tiny body can put up a good fight
against the illness that has entered her otherwise peaceful world.
O Lord, I used to hear parents say
that they would gladly suffer instead of their children,
and now I know what they mean.
I know that our journey here on earth
must include some suffering along the way.
But my instinct is to somehow prevent it.
Help me trust in you during these times,
be a wise guardian of my baby's health,
do all that I can to keep her well,
and know that you are a loving Father
who keeps watch over us all.

Help us appreciate good health when it returns
and rejoice in each day that we are spared illness.
Please send your sweetest angels to comfort
and tend to my baby now as she regains her health and strength.

~

"The LORD nurses them when they are sick and eases their pain and discomfort." —Psalm 41:3

My Journal

~

Yesterday

My mother always comforted me when I was sick by . . .

My Journal

~

TODAY

I take good care of my baby when she's sick by . . .

My Journal

~

Tomorrow

Three things I can do to help my baby stay well are . . .

Calling All Angels!

All through the Bible, Lord,
your angels offer protection, encouragement, advice,
and all sorts of help in times of need.
Please send your angels to watch over our baby.
I ask for the sweetest, most tender angels
to minister to her when she is sick.
The strongest and swiftest angels to protect her
when we are away from home.
The wisest and most patient angels to help her
in the lifelong learning process.
The purest and holiest angels to bring her ever closer to you, O God.
And, finally, I ask the angels who protect and guide all mothers
to be with me today and always.
Thank you, Lord, for all your magnificent angels.

~

"Praise the LORD, you angels of his, you mighty creatures who carry out his plans, listening for each of his commands. Yes, praise the LORD, you armies of angels who serve him and do his will!"
—Psalm 103:20-21

My Journal

YESTERDAY

When I was a child, my favorite story about angels in the Bible was . . .

My Journal

~

TODAY

Lord, help me be ever aware that your angels may be here to help us in the most unlikely places, such as . . .

My Journal

~

TOMORROW

Help me to always remind my child to seek the help of holy angels in the years ahead by . . .

Part Three

All My (Unasked) Advisors

When you're a new mother, Lord, the world is full of advisors.
Everyone wants to tell me what to do. Often I feel so insecure.
Each person is convinced that her way of raising children is best.
Help me not to tune out all sentences starting with,
"What I always did was. . . ."
Remind me that most advice is well-intentioned.
Remind me that those sharing ideas with me
only want to help me do a better job.
Remind me that I often give advice, too.
Remind me that I may learn something of value.
Remind me to keep my sense of humor.
Lord, help me listen openly and patiently to all sincere advice.
Let me consider all the suggestions, evaluate them,
and then find ways to apply ideas that may make life better for me and my child.
Guide me in finding the path that is uniquely my own,
as I try to learn from those who have walked this family path before me.
And always, Lord, remind me that you are my ultimate Advisor.

~

"I rejoice in your word like one who finds a great treasure."
—Psalm 119:162

"Get all the advice and instruction you can, and be wise the rest of your life." *—Proverbs 19:20*

My Journal

~

YESTERDAY

The best advice I received when I was growing up was . . .

My Journal

~

Today

When I need good advice, I know I can rely on . . .

My Journal

~

Tomorrow

The best advice I can give a new mother is . . .

Sharing Your Love

God of all creation, whenever we share with another living creature
we are doing your will.
You shared with us the greatest gift of all — life.
Every day you share your love, peace, and blessings with those who ask.
I want to teach my child to share naturally and willingly.
It all starts with that first rattle passed to another tiny, sticky hand.
Then a cookie, broken and offered with a smile.
Help me to show through my own example the rewards of sharing,
the pleasure of giving to another,
the natural reflex of sharing even the simplest things
such as a smile, a handshake, a hug.
Teaching my child to share is one of the greatest lessons I can offer her.
As I go about this task each day, Lord,
please stay with me and show me all the ways
I can demonstrate the gift of sharing.

A child who truly learns to share will be well on the way to becoming a happy and well-adjusted adult. I fervently pray for this gift from you to my child.

~

"They should be rich in good works and should give generously to those in need, always being ready to share with others what God has given them." —1 Timothy 6:18

"Teach me your ways, O LORD, that I may live according to your truth!" —Psalm 86:11

My Journal

YESTERDAY

The best example of sharing I recall is . . .

My Journal

~

Today

I can teach my baby to share by doing these things . . .

My Journal

~

Tomorrow

Three things we can do to help our child grow up to be a person who shares willingly and lovingly, as God teaches us, are . . .

She Looks to Me

Lord God, I ask for your guidance
as I seek to teach my child how to live in this world
in harmony with you, herself, and others.
What teaching challenge could be greater?
She is so dependent on me (just as I am dependent on you).
Later on, she will come to me with her musings of "Why? How come?"
Give me the patience to deal honestly with all of her needs and questions.
Show me the way to teach by example.
My actions will thunder above my words,
which are often lost in the din of daily family life.
I pray that most of these actions will be lessons I can be proud to teach.
Help me to grow and learn and wonder about our glorious world,
just as my child does.
She has so much to teach me.
Whenever my child looks to me for answers,
dear Lord,
I look to you.

"We will not hide these truths from our children but will tell the next generation about the glorious deeds of the LORD."
—Psalm 78:4

My Journal

~

YESTERDAY

I've always looked to the following people for guidance, support, and advice . . .

My Journal

~

TODAY

Whenever I have questions about raising our child, I know I can always ask . . .

My Journal

~

Tomorrow

I plan to be a good source of advice and encouragement for my child by . . .

Plain Wonderful

Each day can delight us, Lord,
if only we are open to the wonderful, ordinary things around us.
Our children know this.
They thrill to a helicopter that suddenly whirls high over our yard.
They enjoy every slurp of that drippy ice cream cone,
savoring it completely in the "now."
Help us to learn from the children this ability to fully participate
in what we are doing, seeing, feeling, learning.
Is it only the very young and the very old
who hold this precious secret within them?
Savoring the smallest of life's pleasures
can brighten the rich texture of even a so-called ordinary day.
Guide us on this journey of discovery
into fully appreciating the simplest of things
so that we may also guide our children
in never losing their wondrous, wide-eyed approach to life.
Thank you, Lord, for the ordinary.

~

"This is the day the LORD has made. We will rejoice and be glad in it." —Psalm 118:24

My Journal

Yesterday

Some of the plain, ordinary things I have appreciated in the past are . . .

My Journal

~

TODAY

These are a few of the simple pleasures of new motherhood that I give thanks for today . . .

My Journal

TOMORROW

I want to encourage my child to take pleasure in the ordinary and develop an "attitude of gratitude" by . . .

Dreams and Schemes

What were your dreams for this world, God the Creator?
Did you envision your people living and working in harmony,
sharing with one another,
and constantly expressing their love and appreciation for you?
A mother has so many dreams for her child, Lord.
All-knowing Father, you alone can read our innermost desires.
We envision accomplishments both for ourselves and our children.
We see growth and achievement, fulfillment and success ahead.
When we dream, Lord, help us bolster our dreams
with preparation and determination.
Don't let our dreams fade into fantasies.
We want our children to dream, too,
about taking the talents you gave them
and using them fully and freely for your glorification.
When our children's dreams don't conform to our own,
give us the wisdom to encourage them,
even though the path winds somewhere we have never walked before.
If they take a detour, that's all right, too.
Help us remember that our life here is a pilgrim's journey of discovery.

If we are to achieve our dreams, Lord,
help us to appreciate them and be grateful for your help.
If you have chosen other dreams for us to fulfill,
help us accept your will with gratitude.
Help us, Lord, in pursuing our individual dreams,
to bring about your dreams for a peaceful, grateful world.

~

"He always stands by his covenant — the commitment he made to a thousand generations." —*Psalm 105:8*

"Then God looked over all he had made, and he saw that it was excellent in every way." —*Genesis 1:31*

My Journal

~

YESTERDAY

When I was a girl, I often dreamed of doing . . .

My Journal

~

TODAY

My plan for making the most of each day of this first special year includes . . .

My Journal

TOMORROW

I hope that when you grow up you will become . . .

My Prayer for the World's Children

When I became a mother, Lord,
I was reawakened to all the harsh realities of our world.
Overnight, I was filled with a desire to "make it all better."
How can I send this vulnerable child into a broken world
full of hatred, prejudice, violence, disease, poverty, pollution, and drugs?
Help me turn this concern into action.
What can I do in my small corner of the world
to help ease even one of these pressing problems?
How can I use the talents you have given me to benefit my child
and all the children of parents throughout the world?
Show me the way, Lord.
My actions seem so limited, and the problems so enormous.
Please don't allow me to become discouraged.
Help me remember that it isn't necessarily the solution that is important,
but the struggle to achieve it.
My responsibilities are many now,
and my time is more limited than ever before.
Yet if I can put just a small part of my time and energy
into working for a better world,
I will be serving the needs of my child in the best possible way.

I know so many other parents feel this same desire
to make the world a better place for their children to live.
Please show them the way to respond, too, Lord.
If parents throughout the world work together
to protect our environment, eradicate disease, promote peace, alleviate poverty,
think of all we can accomplish!
Help parents everywhere to extend their natural instinct
to protect their own children to all the world's children.
And please protect, guide, and encourage us,
the parents, who are your children, Lord.
Amen.

~

"LORD, you alone are my inheritance, my cup of blessing."
—Psalm 16:5

"So you see, it isn't enough just to have faith. Faith that doesn't show itself by good deeds is no faith at all — it is dead and useless."
—James 2:17

My Journal

~

YESTERDAY

A problem that I worked with others to help solve was . . .

My Journal

~

TODAY

One small step that I can take right now to help children where I live is . . .

My Journal

~

Tomorrow

I plan to show my support for programs and organizations that help children by simple acts such as writing letters, making a few phone calls, and . . .

Happy Birthday!

Lord, as we prepare to celebrate our baby's first birthday,
I look back on this busy, exhausting, exhilarating year.
How quickly the months have unfolded,
each bringing major changes in the baby's growth and development.
One year old! It's hard to believe.
We'll have a birthday cake with one bright candle.
There will be a present or two,
new playthings to fascinate for awhile and then lose their appeal.
O Lord, this is just one reminder
that all the gifts of this world are temporary.
They beckon and gleam like gold, enticing us to own them.
Yet all are destined to fade into the background of our lives,
as new shiny objects replace them.
How thankful we are that we have the one and only lasting gift —
faith in you and the promise of salvation.
This is the greatest gift I'll ever give my child.
The gift of faith will last a lifetime to guide him safely home.

Now let's blow out the candle and make a wish.
A wish that the tiny seed of faith will take root and blossom
within our child throughout his life.
Thank you, Lord, for this perfect birthday gift.

~

"Let each generation tell its children of your mighty acts."
—Psalm 145:4

My Journal

~

YESTERDAY

The most memorable birthday I've ever had was . . .

My Journal

TODAY

Looking back on your first year of life, I thank God for these things . . .

My Journal

~

Tomorrow

Each year on your birthday I'd like to continue the family tradition of . . .

The Days Ahead

God of faithfulness, help me to be steadfast
in my commitments to this child you have entrusted to me.
Help me persist in raising him to be
a person who will reflect your glory
through trying times and joyful occasions,
through ordinary days and extraordinary challenges.
Please give me the gift of quiet persistence.
Help me not to be overwhelmed by the demands
on my time, talents, and patience.
Help me keep all things in proper perspective
as my child and I travel together
on this path of growth and development.
I know that with your help, all of this is possible.

~

"Then I will always sing praises to your name as I fulfill my vows day after day." —Psalm 61:8

My Journal

~

YESTERDAY

Commitments that I have faithfully kept in the past include . . .

My Journal

Today

Raising a child to honor commitments isn't easy in a world that doesn't always value commitment, so I will use examples such as . . .

My Journal

~

Tomorrow

One of the ways I can help my child value and understand commitment is . . .

Our First Good-Bye

O Lord, I am crying tears of both joy and sadness.
My toddler just took his first steps away from me and into the wider world.
He is entering a nursery school that I have carefully chosen,
that is highly recommended, and yet, and yet . . .
My first impulse is to run after him and hold him close.
To protect him from all dangers, both real and imagined.
To keep him to myself just a little while longer.
Will I always have this impulse, Lord?
To encourage new experiences and growth
and still keep everything the same
in a safe, secure environment of my making?
He clings to me for just a while, then happily joins the other children.
I am filled with pride.
Yet I look down the years and see this
as just the first of so many good-byes:
off to school, college, moving away.
Help me always remember that my job as a mother is
to lovingly prepare him for a life of independence, guided by you.
I want to hold on, but I must gently push him
onto the path of his own unique journey.

Good-bye. I love you.
God keep you in the Lord's loving care
and send the holy angels to watch over you.
And, all through your journey,
know that there is always a safe harbor wherever I am.
So it really isn't good-bye.
With God's help, it is only "so long" until we meet again.

~

"But I have stilled and quieted myself, just as a small child is quiet with its mother. Yes, like a small child is my soul within me."
—Psalm 131:2

"See how very much our heavenly Father loves us, for he allows us to be called his children, and we really are!" —1 John 3:1

My Journal

~

Yesterday

I can see now that my parents prepared me to become an independent person by . . .

My Journal

~

TODAY

As a parent preparing a child to live a godly life in this complex world, my prayer today is that . . .

My Journal

~

Tomorrow

Three things that I can do to help develop independence in my child are . . .